WELLWATER

KAREN SOLIE

PICADOR

First published 2025 by House of Anansi Press Inc.

First published in the UK 2025 by Picador
an imprint of Pan Macmillan
The Smithson, 6 Briset Street, London EC1M 5NR
EU representative: Macmillan Publishers Ireland Ltd, 1st Floor,
The Liffey Trust Centre, 117–126 Sheriff Street Upper,
Dublin 1, D01 YC43
Associated companies throughout the world
www.panmacmillan.com

ISBN 978-1-0350-4818-2

Copyright © Karen Solie 2025

The right of Karen Solie to be identified as the
author of this work has been asserted by her in accordance
with the Copyright, Designs and Patents Act 1988.

All rights reserved. No part of this publication may be reproduced,
stored in a retrieval system, or transmitted, in any form, or by any means
(electronic, mechanical, photocopying, recording or otherwise)
without the prior written permission of the publisher.

Pan Macmillan does not have any control over, or any responsibility for,
any author or third-party websites referred to in or on this book.

1 3 5 7 9 8 6 4 2

A CIP catalogue record for this book is available from the British Library.

Printed and bound in Great Britain by Bell & Bain Ltd, Glasgow

This book is sold subject to the condition that it shall not, by way of
trade or otherwise, be lent, hired out, or otherwise circulated without
the publisher's prior consent in any form of binding or cover other than
that in which it is published and without a similar condition including
this condition being imposed on the subsequent purchaser.

Visit **www.picador.com** to read more about all our books
and to buy them. You will also find features, author interviews and
news of any author events, and you can sign up for e-newsletters
so that you're always first to hear about our new releases.

KAREN SOLIE grew up in southwest Saskatchewan. Her five previous collections of poetry – *Short Haul Engine, Modern and Normal, Pigeon, The Road In Is Not the Same Road Out* and *The Caiplie Caves* – have won the Dorothy Livesay Poetry Prize, Pat Lowther Award, Trillium Book Award and the Griffin Poetry Prize, and been shortlisted for the Derek Walcott Prize and the T. S. Eliot Prize. A 2023 Guggenheim Fellow, she teaches half-time for the University of St Andrews in Scotland and lives the rest of the year in Canada.

Also by Karen Solie in Picador

The Caiplie Caves

Also by Karen Solie

The Road In Is Not the Same Road Out
The Living Option: Selected Poems
Pigeon
Modern and Normal
Short Haul Engine

In memory of Howard Solie

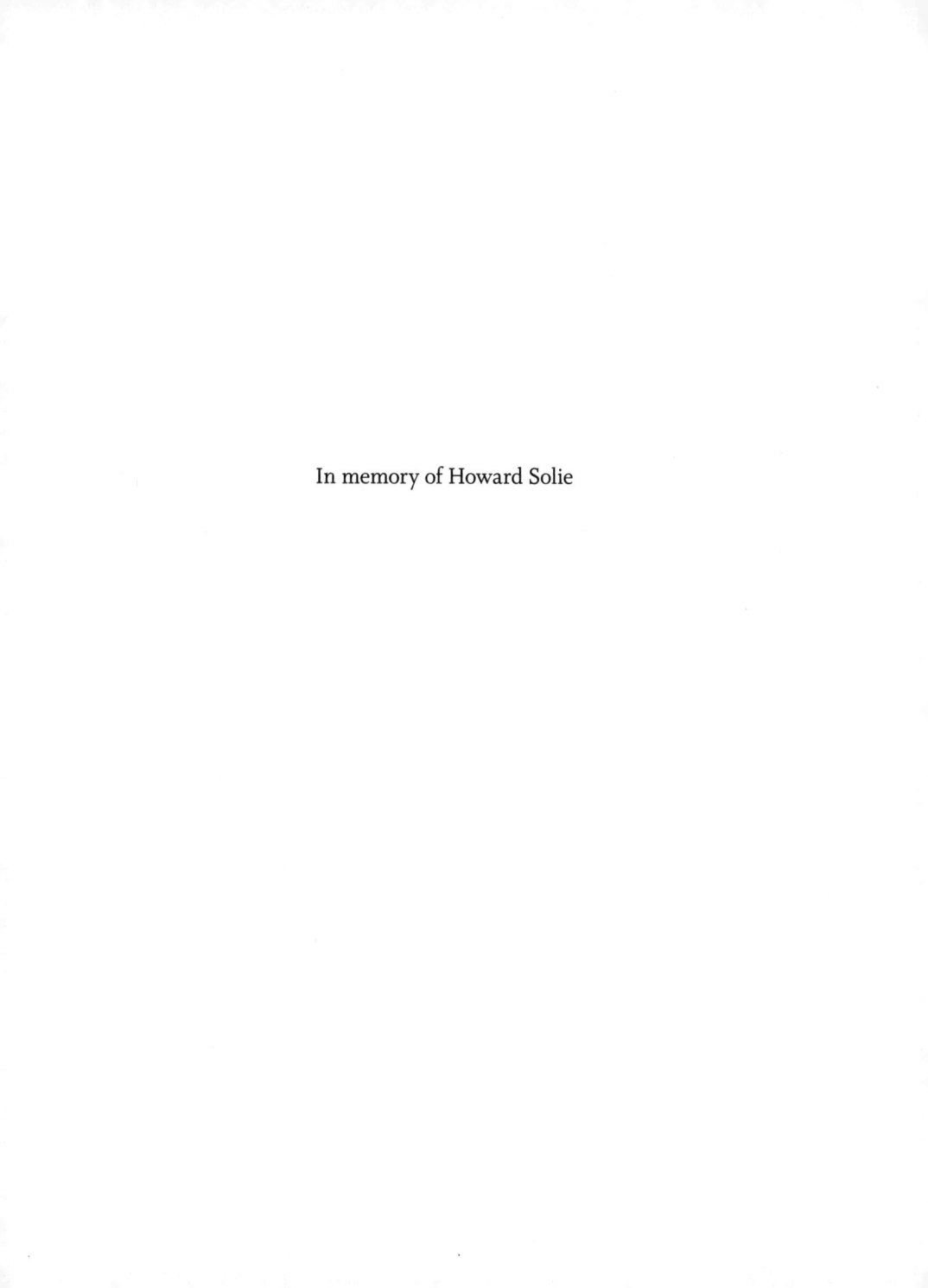

CONTENTS

Basement Suite	3
Wellwater	5
The Trees in Riverdale Park	6
That Which Was Learned in Youth Is Always Most Familiar	8
Bad Landscape	10
Red Spring	11
Autumn Day	17
Toronto the Good	18
Possible Confounding Influences	21
On Faith	22
Parables of the Rat	25
Las Cruces	28
Next Life	31
Dust	32
Caribou	35
The Bluebird	37
Just Say the Word	39
The Snowplow	41
No One's Gonna Love You More than I Do	43
Foxes	45
The Climbing Vine	47
The Mash	49
Yarrow	52
Mourning Doves	54
Flashlight	56
Horseshoe	58

Delisle	60
The Grasslands	63
Antelope	69
Smoke	70
Berkeley Hills, 2022	72
Anne Dufourmantelle	73
Mirrors	75
Lilac	77
Holiday at the Wave Pool	78
The Barrens	80
Prime Location	82
Pines	84
Orion	85
Meadowlark	88
Starcraft	89
Canopy	90
Notes	93
Acknowledgements	97

WELLWATER

BASEMENT SUITE

Left to our use are the fixtures and appliances
repented of by the homeowners
who don't realize this is a way to know them.

In the basement one is closer to God because
closer to consequence, to creatures no one loves
but the specialists. Bean weevil,

rice weevil, rose weevil, pea weevil,
flour, black vine, and strawberry weevils,
a weevil to every purpose under heaven.

The basement is a treehouse in the roots,
think of it that way,
and cold on five sides, like childhood,

when water in the pipes was a talking animal
and it was advertised that soil neutralized
the toxins applied to it

as our bodies did, and that the sea
carried poison on its back into the hills.
Our faces to the wall, to domestic passages

beyond it, where heartbeats and adjustments
are attenuated through the half space, lo-fi,
all light is radio light.

The house tries to forget we are here,
yet there are bars on the windows
in some places, like childhood.

A slight clinging smell is associated.
Every living situation has one.
It's not the underworld for Christ's sake,

which is everywhere, without depth; still,
the gaze does learn to creep along the baseboards
and sharpen its knives on them.

On the surface again, if we can bear it
after so long sheltering
in place, we may appreciate

more than most a bit of natural warmth,
though money flows no more freely up here,
look around you.

WELLWATER

I didn't know what I had,
drove the watertruck underage to the well
in a swimsuit, anointed with baby oil
to encourage a uniform exposure,
a mild burn atop the tank as it filled
in that burgeoning era of means
to an end. It was a chore
to attend this site of worship
from which song was drawn to feed the souls
of planted trees not native to that place,
as we were not native to that place,
our glyphosate on the wind, our malathion,
dust of gravel roads that bore vehicles
of gas well company agents,
fracking derricks across the county
appearing before, as we said, we knew it.
Blondie tore a strip off the wheatfield,
the tank cooled as the level rose,
and I descended to start the engine
so the radio wouldn't drain the battery —
a mistake I'd made and lived to regret,
which is the only way I ever learn anything.
It took 75 minutes. The things you remember.
My last act before closing the tap
to take the hose by the neck and drink,
taste the cathedral's rock and temperature,
the water hard and the table high.
The water then, you could still drink it.

THE TREES IN RIVERDALE PARK

Diagonal paths quadrisect a square acre
white as the page in February.

In the soil of this basic geometry
ash, elm, and maple thrive like understandings
whose bare logics are visible,
understandings the theorem has allowed.

Between roam bodies of the sensible world —
people, dogs, all those lovers
of the material and immaterial

illumined, as under working hypotheses,
by sodium bulbs whose costly inefficiencies
Los Angeles and Philadelphia have apparently
moved on from.

The trees are grand hotels closed for the season.
But belowground, social life is taking place.

As when snow lay on the fields
and people descended to rec rooms, secret bars
like the Snake Pit in the basement of the curling rink
in Golden Prairie. Our big Ford nosing the siding,

we waited for our parents with the engine running,
under grave instruction,

as radio sent our autonomy bounding toward us,
chilling scenarios inspired by the trucking forecast
and news items from Great Falls or Bismarck
freely imagined, songs that gave us bad ideas
and the seeds of a mythology. Ten minutes

then one hour, two,
pop and chips and the gift of the periphery.

I've never understood what 'starlit' means.
On a clear night in their millions
they cast no discernible light

into the dark expanse where a farmhouse sat
sleepless in its chair, and grid roads and bullshit caragana
disappeared, where the animals' lives played out,
smells travelling slowly, low to the ground.

In Riverdale Park the diagonal walks like diagrams
may be said to describe themselves,

which is a relief.
Now snow is blowing through the theorem
that the understandings broadly accommodate,
and sensible bodies adjust their collars to,

bare spots left by departed cars demonstrating
how the outlines of loss might gradually alter

as experience is filled in by its representation,
even if not made peace with.

THAT WHICH WAS LEARNED IN YOUTH IS ALWAYS MOST FAMILIAR

for Erik

Returning from a walk through the fields
in the dirty realism of early spring,
he ran up beside me and said *Auntie,
do you know what?* And I said *What,*

    expecting a load of nonsense about cartoons,
    trucks, the dog, or the recitation
    of a poorly communicated half truth
    misheard in school, having never believed children possess

        an essential knowledge or intuition
        that age, like water, like wind, erodes,
        in ignorance recast as innocence
        by all the insipid diocese of wellness

            in spite of the very obvious reasons
            our factory settings are reprogrammed,
            and the sooner the better, actually,
            I've been a child —

But he said *Auntie, I think there are two kinds of shapes.
Replaceable and irreplaceable shapes.
Triangles, circles, squares, we can make them. But this*
— he held a clod of earth —

is an accident. Will never happen again.
He threw it to the gravel
where it shattered in a rhetorical flourish
of one example made various

and each, he promised, singular.
He's five. And not even I,
who would sooner be right than happy,
could argue.

BAD LANDSCAPE

I can't make it right. Not the shadow lying on the snow,
not the snow, terrain sloping crudely toward
the poor outcome of a structure neither representational
nor abstract, and the sketched-out town beyond
ill-proportioned, depthless, and basic. There isn't any sense
of an *origin*, of what Plato called the lower soul,
to animate what's lacking with the spark of its remainder.
Better than this were the products of by-numbers kits
hanging on the walls of my grandparents' home —
bird dogs, game birds —
that knew what they were, spoke at least of a steady hand
and pride in the completion of a task
for its own sake. Above the roar of the new gas furnace
installed in the living room, as there was no basement,
the volume of the brand new colour television we were warned
to keep our distance from as children. Blue light
of the programs on our faces, some of the outside
was already on the inside, the radiation we were told
was everywhere — power lines, radios, fluorescent light, telephones —
in all of what emitted that low hum of menace
we had no other word for.

RED SPRING

Turbulence over the prairie in May, heat rising

from the just-sown fields. Warmth has unbound the soil,

and from above, lakes, rivers, sloughs

appear as holes in the cloth of settlement, and another world

at play underneath, where *no colonist*

Mastered the wild earth; no land was marked, none parcelled out,

runoff sparkling in the ditches if the snow

fell this year, no joy in winter without snow, no joy

in spring. Through last year's chem fallow, the first raw

leaves unfold, the infant snub-nosed coleoptile

climbs from the cradle of the GMO seed patent,

the earliest stage at which herbicides

may be applied — Luxxur™ for problematic grass weeds —

as white-tailed fawns sleep inside wild chokecherry

in hollowed-out rooms a man can stand up in.

Ask at the mansions of the skies

for rain, and at the all-important tillering stage

apply fertilizer, insecticide, Buctril M™

to which there is no confirmed resistance in Canada, Infinity FX™

for chem-resistant volunteers.

By the power of Bayer (née Monsanto), the chemical

is wedded to the seed. They are literally

made for each other. There is no going back. Yet still

nature lurks within the soil

and the weeds jump up unbidden, each year a little smarter

and more vigorous, with the high-pitched optimism

of adaptation, sinking their anchors into the deep

and banging their empty cups on the table

— foxtail, cleavers, sow thistle, kochia —

and new beetles arrive from the south with their briefcases,

new viruses, fusarium head blight

against which are deployed the foliar fungicides

— Prosaro™, Folicur™ —

and at booting the critical growth regulators

as crop insurance yield-loss coverage begins

lest the scant moisture fail the barren sands

at the very emergence of inflorescence, a delicate phase prone

to environmental stress, aren't we all,

full of oil, blood, systemic glyphosate

advertised as non-persistent; but tell that to DeWayne Johnson

and his non-Hodgkin lymphoma,

ask the crew boss who cleared the nozzle of my sprayer

by blowing through it, they can't go back.

I was given no mask and threw up for six hours.

So strong is custom formed in early years.

I'm sorry, I can't make this beautiful.

Bayer (and formerly Monsanto) admits no wrongdoing,

even with 9.6 billion reserved to settle

pending litigation, another 1.25 to address

future litigation, its proprietary gene technology whispering

in the ears of grain ripening through

its early, middle, and late milks. The chemical

in the field respects the gene, and the farmer the authority

of Bayer (and formerly of Monsanto)

who will not hesitate to make of you an example

if you insult its canola patent by growing your own seed.

Such wide confusion fills the countryside,

it's said you can't go back. Unless you're rich enough

to farm years at a loss, you can't. Corporations buy the land

of those who die or move, and so assembles the hidden machinery of our lives: the feedlots, gas wells, sweatshops, coal mines.

We don't like to think too much about it —

Bayer in our kitchens, in our bread,

as we are its kitchen, the heart of its home, and if we can afford

a nine-dollar loaf of artisan organic ancient grain sourdough

it lives in us too because of those who cannot. When in

its grey facilities, Bayer (and formerly Monsanto)

engineers its terminator seeds, suicide seeds

of a zombie technology, a plant more dead than alive,

and when it patents what it promises not to use, do we believe it?

Can we go back? Meet each other in the old knowledge?

I don't know how to make this beautiful,

though when the wind trails its fingers through the durum

it is, and a day's work is measurable by the eye,

when antelope walk the hills at dusk like grass-fed spirits

from the otherworld, before the grid,

when the ancient science of a cover crop of yellow sweet clover

or alfalfa sings into the air a fragrance

drawing to itself the fragile pollinators,

butterflies, ladybugs, and the bees to their harvest —

the colony come forth to sport and play

so deep their love of flowers —

it's beautiful, when sleeping populations open their eyes

and nitrogen is fixed inside the earth.

AUTUMN DAY

We queue to manage the balances of what we're owed
to what we owe, orderly as souls in private panic before the Judgement,
shuffling our documents as though judgement weren't already written
in the Cloud. From the shop adjacent wafts the incense
of coffee and the vulgar muffins, overstuffed as geese
with funnels down their throats, truly the muffins of a culture on the brink
of steep decline. To be no longer working bodes differently
for those of us who will not walk, as in the promotional literature,
upon the equatorial beaches, will never point excitedly
to the castles of Europe. Money buys the knowledge it isn't everything.
With the face of a poet no longer young and the manner
of a registered nurse, a customer service representative
translates the truth of our condition to a language even we
can understand: *Whoever has no house now, will never have one.*

TORONTO THE GOOD

Six-inch all-caps in the third-floor window
of a low-rise on Sherbourne. HORRIBLE LANDLORDS.

STAY AWAY. THEY TREATED US LIKE DOGS.
Like a plague cross on the door:

Lord have mercy upon us.
Why don't they move then?

You know why.
If you don't, you should.

Rent for those apartments wed
to flakeboard, caulkstrip, Mactac, plastic,

and a maintenance philosophy
of who gives a shit,

for the ill-intentioned micro-suites, the bug-ridden
and the windowless,

has doubled in two years.
I loved it here.

Even the stodgy Upper Canadian Presbyterian
architecture, the terrifying Ballardian subway

it took me ages to get used to. The parade
of baffling flats we viewed, advertised as 'funky,' 'quirky,'

were tiny museums of illegality
we convinced ourselves weren't bad.

They were our homes.
Then came the renovictions. Airbnb. Friends,

you would weep to see the faucets,
custom cabinets, subway tile, to-code wiring and ventilation

deemed wasted on us lot.
Across the street from Victoria Park

where the Homeless Memorial recites its many deaths
— four this year, and it's January —

New City Hall's functionalist aesthetic now seems witlessly
ironic, like dressing as a miner or a maid for Halloween.

One might be forgiven, hearing old age approach
as a rustling in the dry goods,

cold wind of the institution
whistling through the frame of a cheap slab door,

for not wanting to be around when it arrives,
for crawling back to sleep or to wherever

fear can't follow.
Nearing the courthouse, Old City Hall,

its red sandstone sourced from the Credit River Valley,
I declined the invitation of a passerby to smile.

When he spat at my shoe,
called me a cunt, if I'd risen to it

(should I have risen to it?),
it would have felt like being young again.

POSSIBLE CONFOUNDING INFLUENCES

A drop ceiling full of old fluorescents burning through the night
in a decommissioned Sears; a flower wall of live outlets;
the aural equivalent of acrylic or Elizabeth Arden M
by Mariah Carey — diagnosing the origin of my symptom,
four doctors with cameras and lights retreat into a mist of advice

about hormones. I am my own bee-loud glade
in the bright meadow of the symptom, beyond the limits
of the medical catchment area, the significance, nuance,
and sheer volume of the symptom at the centre of rotation
like the sun. Experience is not reducible to mechanisms, surely:

so why am I at the front desk describing the noise in my room
in the middle of the night — unbalanced laundry, plumbing seizure,
self-destructive industrial fan — and assured with all the sincerity
of the brand that never in the annals of collective experience
have staff ever fielded such dire complaints about room 207,

that room 207 has heretofore only been received as restful
if not downright restorative, its vibrations those of deep
healing, self-acceptance, and inner peace, that if anything
it is an invitation to the adventure of my being; but, ma'am,
if you'll have a seat over there, we'll see what we can do.

ON FAITH

There was no reason
not to believe
the overgrown wells
in abandoned yards

still held water
that, like all things forsaken,
was ruined and dangerous.
But poor Debbie, I thought,

at the Ice Capades with our mothers
in the Medicine Hat Arena,
when the skater
struck her pose in our corner

and Debbie insisted
She's smiling at me!
The hypnotist
we saw there as a family

through emanations
of cigarette smoke and suede
sought to meet with his voice
each inner eye,

counted down from ten
and a handful of souls
in the audience rose
and began to sing

Happy Birthday as he said
the openhearted would.
Our laughter had the prestige
of pity in it.

His post-hypnotic suggestion
that for the rest of their lives
when they heard
that song, those singers

would be filled with joy
and calm, though —
that shut us up.
Five years later

ringside at the cage match
with three friends and a bottle
of cherry whisky
I watched The Stomper

bite the blood squib
as Bret 'The Hitman' Hart
shoved his face into
the steel mesh

and a woman behind us
stood up and screamed
I love you Bret
now finish him off!

PARABLES OF THE RAT

I

The rat and I, we are like brothers.
He, with his knowledge of causes,
the elder, and my weakness

the burden he shoulders.
I see him in shadow, a drink
in his hand, retreating to his rooms

with a bad sandwich, slipping in
at all hours, his brown coat's collar
turned up, somewhere between

a soldier and a criminal.
In the eyes of God and society,
which are the same eyes,

he's succeeded wildly, but not properly;
and one day, in the house
of his labour, he'll ingest the poison

of the family order, and everything
he's seen and heard me do
will die with him.

II

An abstract made of material that may
or may not be invisible,
the universe expanding into infinite space
inheres in rats, in germs, in leaves.
In the largest of us to the least
all its relationships are to scale.
Like it or not, at birth, it's what we're given.

And maybe a soul is a satellite,
a small idea orbiting a larger one, a device
to translate a signal
and send it back.

The rat is still a rat.
There is no getting around what we are.

In a picture book I owned as a child
a girl at camp was assigned a tent
filthy, broken-down, and tiny,
off to the side of those of the popular girls
arranged in shining rows. *Don't be sad,*

said her friend, a witch, who may or may not
have been invisible. *Close your eyes. Go in.*
And inside was a mansion of many rooms
filled with what we all want.

The last shall be first. I remember this too.
But sometimes the last stay last.
Maybe the mind of the rat is a palace.

III

Nevertheless, rat, you can't live here.
Your habits aren't compatible
with our plans for our interiors,

just as our habits render uninhabitable
whatever bit of the whole wide world
we can squeeze our heads into.

The traps are laid, though I didn't lay them.
Nor, when it's time, will I be the one
to carry your body out.

I don't want it to happen. Still, I imagine
as to all animals whose bones
in our hands become garbage,

it will. Rat, unlike you I'm ashamed
of what I do, which is nothing.

LAS CRUCES

A shadow crawls along the arris
like Giovanni Maria de Agostini, like the need
of Giovanni Maria de Agostini
light tries to avoid.
      Our time together nears its end;
and so I hesitate to mention
two dreams of mine
that have come true. One literally,
one figuratively, the one
I'm living now.
      In the early '90s, God help us,
we drove from Austin to New Mexico,
the dry counties, I'm ashamed to say our inquiries
north from Midland were endless
to Lubbock, which did not engender
an inclination to die to self.
In our morning's suffering at Texico
B— found a snake, a black-necked snake,
against the wall of Red's Border Town Playorama,
said he'd get what lay in the glove box to kill it
but it was harmless and afraid.
      I had always pitied the snake
beneath the foot of the Blessed Virgin,
it looked to me vulnerable to misrepresentation,
but B— said enmities
had been established between them, that purity
is not a passive quality, and Mary, like the bride
in the Song of Songs, is bright as the sun,

lovely as the moon,
yet terrible as an army with banners flying,
and we argued all the way to Santa Rosa,
through Clovis, Melrose, up the 84
into the valley of Lake Sumner.
  A—, from the back seat, who rarely spoke,
said that God had failed to protect her. You don't know
what goes on under the stairs of a person
who locates their privacy in self-destruction.
  Somewhere north of Las Vegas we stopped,
near Hermit Peak where B— said they filmed
Red Dawn, not the remake, Father,
and where Giovanni Maria de Agostini
lived in a wound in the side of the Sangre de Cristos
9,000 feet above the Pecos Wilderness
and seemingly immune to the reality principle
delivered sermons, God help us, on luxury and avarice,
and cures made from herbs, roots, leaves,
and water from unknown sources.
Drawn from childhood to a life of solitude,
he could not tolerate the loneliness,
could not choose between them,
  it's like an ecosystem —
if you have centipedes, you don't have cockroaches.
Is it the same?
You tell me.
Not choosing was the switch in his dynamo
from Rome to South America to Canada,
on foot and in boats, his months in Montreal,
he wrote, the saddest
of his life. I shouldn't wonder.

        What compels someone, even someone
whose fact-to-fiction ratio is unclear,
to leave where he is loved for a miserable hole
at the base of the Organ Mountains
to be found with a knife in his back,
silver crucifix in his hand, and the medals
of Our Mother?
A priest was indicted but never tried.
        We never made it to Taos.
Did Giovanni Maria de Agostini not anticipate
the consequences? He'd advised the citizens
of Las Cruces that to not see the fire
at the mouth of his cave come the evening
        (the evening, forgive us)
was to understand that he had perished.

NEXT LIFE

Someone desiring the blue of the sky was sold this earthly
mis-tint, a wall colour that even in daylight feels
threadbare, solitary, a little irritable, possibly lead-based,

a blue that suits a crucifix in pride of place
above the TV on its rolling collapsible metal stand.
It's getting to be about that time to switch the lamps on.

When she died, not much could be passed down. What she owned
worn through the core of its function, in rags
or with the true nature of its construction exposed.

Beloved objects were of no worth
absent of her regard. And it was more than that, as though
the spirit of her belongings, any remnants of utility and charm,

had chosen to accompany her into the next life. The world
used her right up, along with the little she'd been given.
But everything she'd been given she found a use for.

DUST

Returning home from evening mass
in the big car,

they were like canal boats then
sliding through the loose gravel, in the back seat

she pushed my cuticles up
with a silver file, not unpainfully,

to expose the half moons, she said
God put them there, he likes to see them.

An empty bottle rolled under the passenger seat
and back out again

as my grandfather drove,
one foot on the gas, one on the brake,

it was a clear glass bottle with white lettering,
and a sense of the conditional crept in through the vents

like dust, the incense of the road
scrubbing the air of clarity, of all else but the demands of dust,

what you need replaced
with what you don't — you are ignored

by everything as you struggle with it.
I was an empty bottle on the floor

of a church filling with dust,
a flame of dust on the horizon

like the one to which the Sandman gestures, when he says
to the sleepy child at the window, Look,

>*there rides my twin. If, pure of heart,*
>*you've done this day all you might have,*

>*by one of us will you dream of beauty;*
>*and if you have offended*

>*through any of the thousand ways to offend*
>*by the other you will wake from dreams of fear.*

>*But as St. Matthew has advised,*
>*do not be anxious about tomorrow, tomorrow*

>*will be anxious for itself,*
>*sufficient for today is its own trouble, although we can't*

>*really say that anymore can we.*
>*No matter,*

>*because here my brother has arrived*
>*shaking time's dust out of his clothes*

*and isn't he handsome
checking his phone,*

*its screen like the moon
in the eye of his horse.*

CARIBOU

Why, after so many years, is she with me now?
We who were not close in life
walk among the caribou lichen

whose coral-like low forms, white against the mosses
and wild blueberry in its red phase,
seem to give off light.

She has escaped
through the window of the body's house of harm
into the freedom of a truth that will never be recognized.

And indeed they do give off light, fungi and algae
in a collaboration that obscures
the individual collaborators

who've taken it entirely off-spectrum,
reflecting every wavelength and phosphorescing under the UV
intensely where appearing most delicate,

as though, as has been written, the best metaphor for stillness
is constant motion. Out of weakness
are made strong, I guess.

A cold-hardy, slow-growing, clean-air species.
The fog makes surprising
what it does not conceal, and what is concealed reminds us

that an excess of surprise should be avoided, if one can help it.
Listen to the sea, she says,
surprising again and again the rock of the shore.

THE BLUEBIRD

Each old thing in its new place must prove its worth yet again.
Dust is disturbed, having made itself at home

among what former tenants have found wanting.
A friend brings a gift to brighten my room, then leaves

a cruel word to move in with me.
Good and bad don't always line up opposite.

Nearing the end of an earlier journey, I'd stopped at
a roadside motel whose name ameliorated

the experience of staying there
not at all. Around it rose the dark forest of the Shield country,

endless differentiation appearing undifferentiated
though one had the sense of something slowly,

unrelentingly, being taken apart within.
Ahead lay great happiness, great sorrow, and it seems to me now

a decision was to be made between them,
though the conditions for such a choice did not exist.

The past is so poorly constructed, so unsuited to the living
that must be done, we might wish for the forest to grow up around it —

but knowledge can't replace the facts
of its acquisition. They continue to perform

in the events they set in motion
whether we remember them or not.

I was hungry, it was very late. Across the four lanes
northbound, southbound, divided in my memory

by a waist-high steel girder, a gas station convenience store's
neon still awake. Seldom a break in the traffic,

footbridge miles away. To get to the other side quickly
meant taking your life in your hands.

JUST SAY THE WORD

I signed the papers, and the world created out of all I have destroyed
honestly doesn't look much different.
A grainy whitish wind blows in from Little Poland

and a human form in winter upholstery
screams unanswerable questions into traffic. Questions,
while inadequate to truth, are faithful to sorrow, so fair enough.

Inside the padlocked gates of Leal Rental, a grey pitbull shining like a nail
could be the silver dog Argyreos,
and the sun on whose mat of light he sleeps

the gold dog Khryseos,
forged by the god of metalworkers, masons, to guard the threshold
of King Alcinous's legendary hospitality

and its founding principles of order.
I have only ever wanted to see things as they are. Until I did,
and experience narrowed to a fact impossible to turn around in.

Now everything I need to do it myself resides with Leal Rental,
in whose yard a conclave of articulated boom lifts
achieves the conspiratorial symmetry of

The Calling of St. Matthew or *The Supper at Emmaus*,
raised basket platforms attentive, inclined in the manner that indicates
listening, in their posture a hint of nature

aspiring to weightlessness,
and the eye follows the Baroque Diagonal into a sky of vivid, structural
blue, premodern and cloudless.

The craftsman never blames his tools
yet is only as good as they are, which leads
to some uncertainty as to where the fault lies. Argyreos of Leal,

allow me to linger, as I too am between jobs.
A condo development, blocks-long, modular, pre-*démodé*,
has sailed in from an increasingly unaffordable future

flying the skull and crossbones of Tridel Communities.
But it is pleasant to lose oneself on Dupont Street
in the comforting presence of factory colours,

thoughts on their feet high in the thought-baskets
awaiting direction, though from up here
it looks like the whole thing is going to have to come down.

THE SNOWPLOW

The forecast calls for the same ground covered.
In what looks equally like a show of optimism
and of wry futility,
the plow clears the mall's empty lot in a storm —

snow, freezing rain, and fog —
all the measures water takes to avoid certainty
are being taken. The plow is a child of the north,
like Romanticism. And what a dad-rock moment

here on the sidewalk, watching the blade
at its superb angle push everything before it,
old snow with the new, garbage and beer cans

blown from the bus stop, stray carts that will emerge
from greying banks in the melt
awkwardly, like facts undigested by argument.

Standing at a distance with its hands in its pockets,
gradually relinquishing its attachment to retail,
the mall is autonomous as a mind
free from care. Its failures don't bother it.

The moon has shut itself for so long in its attic
above the low ceiling I've forgotten
what phase it's in. Streetlamps stare
from their front steps into the night.

The plow carries away what falls again behind
and this appears peaceful.
Sluggish oil, heated now, runs loosely inside it.

Caution lights illuminate a mist of snow
crystalline and spiritualized,
and if the shadowy operator sees me

he does so from outside my idea of him.
It is the opposite of the intimacy
of a winter interior where a broken understanding
lies quietly on its side.

That the plow is here doesn't mean the worst is over.
I can't speak for the shadowy operator,
but I know he feels the machinery's vibrations
through his bootsoles, in his hands

around the wheel and the controller,
and in his arms, that it activates an expertise
he barely needs to think about.

The engine noise is shoved around by the icy gale,
sometimes it weakens. But it finds me,
as through a crowd going the opposite way.

NO ONE'S GONNA LOVE YOU MORE THAN I DO

The bars have long since closed
when the shouting begins down the street

Open the fucking door

and all the old selves leap to their feet
sick with adrenalin
rushing to the point of convergence
where things go bad.

With momentum and force the voice assumes
a switched-on hydraulic quality
an automatic rosary of no response

a monotony allowing other aspects to intrude
spring night at its coolest just before dawn

the smell of sea fog and late-blooming lilac
the air like the air of a memoir

and in the morning a neighbour comments
You'd think there was a war on.

Or is this just another Friday
in an ongoing Easter of blame and remorse

you in your dark house down the street
creeping through the hallway with your phone
which lights up, begins to ring

and your destiny on the threshold
knocking. Indeed. Pounding.

FOXES

The storm passed though electricity flickered
and stirred-up colour had yet to settle

At the window of the rental with my life half-packed
in shadow I was unseen by them
the city foxes who must always worry
beds unmade, door kicked in more than once

They investigated the fallen beech
its roots exposed like the apartment
of somebody who has died
unable to tidy up first

Stronger trees asleep on their feet
nothing more they could do

and the grass flattened under the book of water
Storm Dennis threw at England

My host would write of me online later
it was as though no one had even been there

Dusk, that untrustworthy time
when holes appear in the civic fabric
and insights are expected to emerge

Characters left over from the séance
tape recordings played through a telephone
double exposures, CCTV photos
two century-old police sketches

when a half door opened at the end
of a darkening corridor they
ran through it

THE CLIMBING VINE

From rocky soil it came
from next to nothing
stretched on the rack of its genome

the pain of its talent running through it
embracing the legs of the decking for comfort

Unidentified   no immediate family
exiled from the chatter of annual plantings
not much in common with the cavalier flowering perennials

Even the sun said   *Whoever you are*
I am not made of money

Everything it owned strapped to its body
arm over arm in its wet clothes
it hauled itself to the second-floor balcony

      and where it spread out   redistributed its weight
like a traveler on a platform

the structure's joints creaked
and the muscles stood out in the nails

Had they let it   it would have scaled the house
      to stand on the roof where God might notice
           what had been accomplished in his absence

Would have torn the house down and stood on the ruin
>   tossing its hook at the downspout of heaven

They pruned it   its strength of conviction redoubled
Cut it back to the trunk
>   a litter of tendrils wobbled out

Razed it to the ground   a shoot appeared
like a prisoner through a manhole
They had to eradicate it at the level of the idea

>   But here ...

THE MASH

On land judged unfit for use

what might appear stagnant is deep in a process

      This Venice of decay

whose superstructure addresses the fog

out of profound humility

      its cellars full of artifacts and medicines

and the roots ticking companionably knitting

the cloth of the bog type and cloth of the fen type

      swamp or marsh   peatlands   muskeg

as many names as exist for hope

for despair

and their sub-forms

      the domed the plateau the basin the blanket

      the riparian the channel the feather and the spring

fruits of which are to be chosen from wisely

      One second on solid ground

the next knee-deep in the mire

you might wonder why it can't decide

land or water

why can't one thing in this life be clear

    As if any of us would want to choose just one thing

Years ago I wouldn't have thought much of it

The rusty blackbird   like an older cousin

    can open anything with a knife

there's drama at street level among

the pitcher plants and sundews

a spicy aroma drifts from windows   sunlight refracts

down through prisms of the vault lights

to where barrels are rolling   linens are being cleaned

    In long rooms sliding under the surface

items are stored and preserved

    I feel the work going on out there sometimes

        hear with my imagination

the soft motors

    air exchange   filtration

    at the spongy and inexact edges of perception

        like the widening ripples where the green frog was

            or scent of blooming spring ephemerals

        Like Dickinson's pond lilies opening

                in the slow-moving water of contemplation

        Like the voices of loved ones from another room

whose absence will wake you

YARROW

The thousand leaves of an old knowledge,
umbels of its inflorescence, conquer the road-edge

and riverbank, it's one of the indecencies of age
that landscape takes on this commemorative aspect.

Achillea millefolium —
though it was Patroclus who used the fernlike analgesic leaves,

hemostatic also and delicately furred,
to treat the wounds of fallen soldiers. With knowledge comes

that duty. Pain, mostly, and the relief from pain.
Duty performed willingly feels like kindness

to its recipients, kindness withheld like cruelty.
Patroclus, well-loved, but a person will follow his nature.

Some answers are so simple they can be awful to look at,
so obvious as to inspire anger, like a monochrome painting

that refuses the existence of any secrets
it might hide from us, that we could fight about

or pretend to ignore. There is no starting over,
never has been. And like an adage the yarrow deteriorates

quickly, yellows, smells like the back end of a festival,
all that wasted potential, while upstream

at Cahill Fabrication, an industry we can all get behind,
another simile detaches from the narrative,

searches for crisis in the action
but finds things resemble most clearly what they are,

if made a little easier to swallow. In pill and tea form
yarrow is prized, yet disapproved of in its natural state

for how it proliferates in a time
when scarcity is a strategy. I would have liked

to offer my kindness as freely to you, when it mattered,
would have liked to think I had it in me.

MOURNING DOVES

Sounds about right, panic shredding
the far edge of the vowel like a flag-end
in relentless wind

and you can't walk ten feet
without branches exploding
in your peripherals, you'd think

creatures so hopeless on the ground
would find their measure of grace in flight
but they rattle and creak like

prototypes, plod up the stairs
of the lower air as though from a train platform
laden with bags, it's awkward, really

painful to look at, the fields and paths
where they rise and are killed and rise
and are killed, but it doesn't

matter, there are so many, I would like
to afford them the respect of neutrality
but I don't want to hear them

anymore, don't want to see their
grey rags dropped from the drying line
grey smoke in the hawthorn tree or

squatting on the eaves like taxidermy
stuffed with personal tragedy
and singing —

> *If I knew a friend on all this earth*
> *you've been a friend to me*

FLASHLIGHT

In bed near the open window
like someone wandered away from a campfire.

When the eyes adjust,
features of the landscape can be discerned

as might the outlines of belief,
no helpful detail within.

When I asked if she'd seen my friend, she said
We don't all know each other in this place

for Pete's sake, death is not Saskatchewan.
It's obvious now where this is going.

Enough, already, about the soul.
But was it not invented out of necessity,

a word for the unnecessary,
as mathematics requires the null set,

as the flashlight rests beside the bed
though you've lived here long enough

to find your way without it?
There's time enough to tell me I'm wrong,

she'll do that later.
The prospect he loved, I see it

and don't see it.
All the things in the night house

as he touches them one by one.
It can be true if you recognize the lie in it, she said.

Far ahead, the stubborn soul of my friend
switches off its flashlight,

lays aside its walking stick.
Soon its hands will be free.

It drinks the last of the water
it no longer needs to carry.

HORSESHOE

Seriously, in all that time, I asked, did your faith never waver?
How unprepared you are for these moments, she said,
even as it might seem

your whole life has been preparing you. And though inclined
to reticence while alive, preferring that events
speak for themselves, she told me a story.

We were gathered, she said, at a long table
beside the lilac trees, the family, and my brother out of hospital.
After supper had finished he recalled

how his former music teacher, a brilliant pianist but a cruel man,
had died, if you can believe it,
when a horseshoe nailed above his door

fell on his head as he crossed the threshold.
Despite my brother's talent, she said,
his teacher told him repeatedly that a person of his emotional delicacy

would never go anywhere.
And, in fact, he didn't.
The horseshoe had once belonged to what many local people considered

the municipality's luckiest horse, who was rescued
after falling through river ice,
and had escaped, miraculously, unharmed,

when lightning struck a tree it was tied to.
When later its cries warned the farmer the barn where it was stabled
had caught fire,

he swore the horse need never work again.
I myself recall this horse, she said,
a sturdy little strawberry roan renowned also for its gentleness.

It lived to a very old age
and died in the meadow it was born in.
My brother's teacher was given its shoe before travelling to the city

for a piano competition, which he won;
the reason, we presumed, why he never again competed.
But I know all this, I said. I heard it, I was there.

A red and white checked oilcloth
was attached with clothespins to the table.
I wore a new sundress I hated, and complained of.

Afterward Uncle laughed and said that none of it was true.
But you weren't there, she said to me
in my dream. Not if I don't remember you.

DELISLE

The name of the village
'of the island'

though the water hid in the ground
and the sea was grass.

There, I was a child.
Around the house in spring

the lilacs bloomed
perfumed and bright as city girls

and winter withdrew all the way back
into purity.

Illness resided there too, under the family name,
a dependent we prayed for

and to, it seemed.
Mother, Father, even little D—, indistinct

as if faded by exposure. But I
was a new soul.

Not a plant in the house
because of the dirt, and as they didn't live long,

no animals, my parents
without the strength, they said,

for my sadness. So nothing was given me, nor
was anything taken. I credit them

for my ability to walk a narrow beam.
And though I looked like someone

who walked a narrow beam, my eyes
were wide, my fear

was wide. At the piano D— appeared
less to play than to act

as the open window
through which music drifts.

The village grew, its streets were paved,
the asphalt melted

then froze and buckled
throughout our young adulthood.

When I married,
D— stayed on alone.

He was made to wait too long.
Then the illness found me too,

began the slow work of carrying me
piece by piece

from one place to the next.
And God was there the whole time.

THE GRASSLANDS

Ghosts if you believe in them. If you don't,
the similarly see-through unquiet miles.

      Is this beauty, all this grass?

Not much of a place for a holiday, not much to do.
A few falling-down farms and a bad history.
No cell service in sections, no GPS,

      and who remembers how to use a compass, where
can you even buy a compass, you are lost
long before you know it.

      Rolling hills
of bouldery glacial moraine,
hunting ground of the nomadic Gros Ventre,
Cree, Assiniboine, Blackfoot, Lakota Sioux,

until settlement — as settlement does,
      without consultation, in violence and paperwork —
by the Dominion Lands Act of 1872

sold semi-arid acreage to immigrant farmers
and the land blew away without the grass to hold it down.

      The best thing for it may be that we are not there —
      But what good is a place left on its own?

Oil and gas companies say, not much.
Grass-covered hill after grass-covered hill
keeping its concerns to itself, and the Frenchman River,

hardly a river,

meandering its tilted valley, muttering about irrigation,
swinging its head side to side like a working horse.

      Parks Canada stretched a map
across all this evasiveness,
pinned the East Block to Rockglen, the West

to Val Marie

      (combined population 521) —

          If you hope to find yourself
in the back country be careful what you wish for
alongside the pure-bred irritable bison,

sylvatic plague in the fleas
and the fleas on the prairie dogs
in the prairie dog town featured in the brochure,

rattler, coyote, black widow spider,
      the water saline, you can boil it all you want.

Quicksand and sinkholes of the Killdeer Badlands,
vertical yards of watery mud —

                    And when you do venture in
with your tire tracks and snake gaiters

the hospitality of grass
is a dry loaf, cracked cup, mattress of prairie wool,
northern bedstraw and great blanket flower,
wild licorice, clover, corn mint, bergamot,

and heat, rippling like curtains
          as the grasshoppers saw away —
                    leave your packed lunch out they will eat it in an hour —

wind and speargrass unpicking your stitches
as the shade level rises in the Otter Basin
and a fragrant interval leans over your bed
like your parents in eveningwear on their way out the door.

                    No one plans for rain
until the rain falls.

On the dirt roads keep your vehicle in sight
when a long-armed leading edge storms the stage
and the water table
pulls lightning from the clouds —

          In winter you might hear
          an elderly grass blade
          shrugging off a shawl of frost,

under the crust the snow's muscles twitching,
a vole clearing her throat,

          but would you bet your life
on your MotoMaster battery,
nowhere to plug in your block heater for a hundred miles

or even to buy
a sandwich, would you believe it —

        Yet, as each inclination aspires to need,
infrastructure ramps up on the National Park lands,
campgrounds and parking lots to explain the perspective,
a reassuring experience of scale, for what good to us
is a place left on its own?

            Be quiet for once. Less
than your own boot print.

On the northern mixed-grass prairie
the kingdom of grass is the kingdom of means:

            the silvery, slender, rough,
    needle-leafed, wavy-leafed, cut-leaf, thyme-leafed,
    wild, false, tufted, and procumbent,
    fringed and nodding, the long-bracted, shaggy,
    pleated, brittle, the creeping and the smooth,
    panicled and pale, common
    and endangered,

            the swift fox, sage grouse, burrowing owl,

    black-footed ferrets
reintroduced, so much else taken —

They belong to themselves as you belong to yourself,
more difficult to restore than to destroy.

                      And what good are you
                      left on your own?

            Unmet at the meeting point, obsessed with endings,
            all the nothing really adding up?

Grasses pass teaspoons of silence
each to each up the slopes of Eagle Butte,

seed heads broadcasting from high broken country
south of the Trans-Canada Highway
a live on-air silence

like the smell of water
a floating inland sea —

                    If not convinced
of your purpose
the grass will not convince you.
What you need to hear you must tell yourself.

           Under the darkest night skies on Earth
an explanation is not forthcoming.

The stars and planets' backs are turned, they are deep
in a conversation of millennia, aurora's weather
hitting the window of the atmosphere

as ice pellets or birdsong, time evaporating
in near-desert conditions,
> your solitude returned to you unopened,

and unable now to see your own hand in front of you,
you are actual size among your equals

> under the twelve constellations
>> the five wild zones of heaven —

ANTELOPE

They appear out of nowhere as if they know where all the doors are
between our dimension and where they are called
by their true name, where they are not the last survivors
of their evolutionary niche. Understanding does not diminish
their curiosity, and even the great plain aligned to the grid of monoculture
is not monotony, which is painful to them,
but a regularity that gives value to change, and WTF is that
walking on the road? How annoying to be drawn into
another pointless encounter with me;
they huff, brandish their hardware and run,
entering a sublimity of motion that is like the sublimity of night.
As a Gothic spirit loves accumulation, magic, a big-block V8
in a Dodge Polara, they feel inside themselves an extra gear
that will lift them from the earth, from the prairie's hall
of mirrors, those fences whitetail leap
that they must scrabble under, tearing their cloaks on the barbs.
Only their old-timey machinery can digest the rough forbs.
The jackrabbit finds peace in her evening hollow, deer fold themselves
in elegant anxiety upon their grass couches, but the pronghorn's eye
has been widened in some back-room occult transaction and he haunts
the open country, a candle in the five-mile corridor of his tenfold vision,
sleeping minutes at a time under the shaking rings of Saturn.

SMOKE

The first morning on waking
I thought it was fog, or mist, I thought it had rained,
but the ground was dry.

The second morning, the sun was red.
At High Level, Fox Creek, the fires uncontained
were borne on the winds they made

and to expand their sphere of influence
they burned a school. The gas and hydrocarbons found us
800 miles south

where the sky was yellow. On the third day, by afternoon,
actions were performed out of duty, not interest.
When the red moon rose we drew the curtains.

Disabused of an illusion we say the fog has lifted,
the smoke has cleared, the dust
has settled, and now we see,

though what arises is not clarity
but a set of new misgivings. Is this how the world will be
and not just how it is?

The blossoming apple shifted key from ode
to elegy, knelt down inside itself in its halo of bees
on the fourth day.

Clearwater River Dene Nation, Island Lake,
Île-à-la-Crosse, 500 miles south
of the evacuations

in the evening of this fifth day, we're advised
to stay out of what the smoke is, its particulate
of houses, plants, animals.

BERKELEY HILLS, 2022

In Wildcat Canyon live the laurels.
No rain in two months and nine days.
Like girls do, the laurels grow
from the soil of a deep reserve.

Inside their frivolity they gather
themselves, still dropping
folded notes onto the others' open books,

though now they are doing it
underground. They cool their feet
in the pool of their own shade.

When a leaf is plucked from one
the others rustle their clothes.

When that leaf is crushed in the hand
its fragrance calls back to the grove.

ANNE DUFOURMANTELLE

I'm through with fiction.
From now on, only fact.

Not the story of a worry stone
that over six decades and an ocean

is carried in the pocket of
a predictably idiosyncratic beauty,

but the mineral composition
of the rock. Not the windswept shore

upon which it is lost. Not the lesson
in letting go; no one

needs reminding. Rather, the name
of the philosopher who wrote that life

begins in risk, who drowned
trying to rescue children

from the current that overwhelmed her.
The children, who were unharmed.

Like a fence that keeps tourists
from the chasm, names

are the nearest we can get
to truth. Bach's twenty children

and what killed the twelve
who pre-deceased him.

Will a novel about it make the whole
miserable business worthwhile?

An escape, some say, from the pain
that owes its life to us, from the imperative

to act. But it's not an escape, is it,
when you know you have to go back.

MIRRORS

She once told me that as a child she fantasized about going into hospital.
It was long ago, hospitals were different.
Still, they are places where people are cared for.

She might have had the wrong idea about hospitals, I don't know,
and maybe about care,
as to care for and to care in practice can diverge.

The Old English *cearian* — 'to grieve,' 'to be anxious,' 'to feel concern' —
originates in the Proto-Germanic *karo*, or 'lament,'
further rooted in the syllable for 'to call out' or 'scream.'

Should those paid to care for us be expected to embody
the extent of this progression, from concern to lamentation?
They truly are like family

in that duty of care is a job one can walk away from,
even if only in the mind.
In Late Latin, *hospitale* is a guest-house or inn.

An alternate evolution of care is represented in the German *karg*,
Dutch *karig* — 'frugal,' 'stingy,' 'scanty,' 'mean.'
Positive applications, 'inclination' or 'fondness,'

seem to have developed later as mirrors to earlier meanings.
And it can take some time to understand what side of the mirror you're on.
Etymology is itself hospitable,

like a brief stay in hospital, somewhere to rest, to recover.
Perhaps basic hospitality was enough for her.
Because if you decide something is enough, it's enough.

LILAC

In the portrait she is in profile
in her chair against the tall window
in browns, she wore a lot of brown,
the light less light than an absence of brown

and the branches of the yard lilacs
without even their simple leaves. Winter then,
or early spring, or the lack
of an artistic capacity for leaves. How sad,

I thought. But why? In silhouette
her finer features are not visible. Yet the portraitist
spent on her, if not talent, at least the attention
that might confirm a person as briefly among the living

even when overwritten as she is here
with another's signature, and the year.

HOLIDAY AT THE WAVE POOL

Warmish, oft-bathed-in, pride
of the second-most visited and largest mall
by gross leasable area
on the northern subcontinent, was it not,
in a childhood when travel meant Edmonton,
astonishing, a wonder of the world?
And on the other side of the intervening years
during which acknowledgment was sought,
sometimes deserved, and occasionally won,
when individuality hardened the heart and mysteries
into problems, is it not a respite from the buses in March,
from all the falling, and soothing to the shoulders
and the knees? Stroll without your heavy coat
along the ice-free corporate boulevards
out of the wind, road salt, the violently arbitrary
real, and get your steps in, you in the light
of your living, you one-off among
the wings' repeating franchises, we of the *just looking, thanks* —
can we dance inside a little to the serviceable pop,
cry when it's sad in front of everybody?
This humour called sorrow is inevitable as the food courts
devoted to each stage of life and corresponding institution.
A water feature beneath potted trees
who've unfocused their eyes forever
is a place to enjoy without buying, like nature.
Pretty decent. It could be worse.
With Mom and newborn brother in hospital,
we left our square of lawn tied to the clothes horse

shivering in back of the duplex and went every night to
McDonald's, my dad, little sister, and me,
him not knowing what else to do with us.
And my god, it was glorious.

THE BARRENS

North Atlantic wind tries
to tear the roof off the hill,
throws all the sea's abrasives at it,

but the tuckamore grew up
in this house, body shaped
by the timeless occupation

of a back bent low, hands
in the dirt, working
at the fasteners.

It's hard to think of anything
more modestly and completely
successful. A forest

of white spruce and balsam fir
centuries old and three feet tall,
its villages of cubbyhole, attic,

and lean-to are home
to the vulnerable thrush,
to the vole who bounces

on its bedsprings, rabbits
lose their keys in its alleys,
even sheep find a nave

in which to say
their panicked rosaries
in a storm; it is you

who are most definitely
not to scale.
All around in the low halls

hurricane lamps are being lit.
To look in the windows
you will have to crawl.

PRIME LOCATION

Many years ago we viewed it
above the shop called simply
Convenience, a luxury
the apartment opposed, its floors

already soft, ceiling convex,
falling into the arms of gravity
as do we all. Vacant now,
it's on the bus route

and so I see it too often,
first tentative tags given way
to bubble and wildstyle climbing
the brickwork, a paste-up of Shiva,

destroyer of worlds,
and the inscription *Fuck Landlords*.
As radiation accelerates the evolution
of the feral dogs of Chernobyl,

greed and neglect have hastened
the building's transition
into a state beyond purpose.
The land beneath it has its ear,

it inhales the amnesia
of spores, light filters through
its soaped windows like light
through the soaped windows

of all the deconsecrated churches
awaiting resurrection as condos
with paradisical walk scores.
They are released for a time

into a common meadow. But Denise is right:
"Your past can't tell it *is*
the past," and won't go gently.
When a mysterious and purifying fire

prepares *Convenience* for demolition,
another trace of us will vanish
with it, one less excuse
for sentimental nonsense, in this life

one has to be hard. Honestly,
it can't happen fast enough.
And the owner will say it's for the best,
he couldn't give that place away.

PINES

The Norfolk pine, in distress, has shed
its lower limbs, as though climbing itself
out of a crisis likely of water or light.

Under its pot, the wood floor is unfaded
but worse off for going unseen, split by water
that's excited a weakness, water one of the things

that can damage a structure while leaving it
mostly intact. You need to understand damage
in order to communicate it simply

to the adjusters, assessors, investigators,
the extent of it. Some songs are so simple
you don't recognize at first how good they are,

how difficult to play. Huddie Ledbetter called that
feeling. So simple it will scare you to death.

ORION

Smoking in the yard two weeks before Christmas
out of the wind, under Orion,
inhaling anger, exhaling sorrow,
which is how anger metabolizes,
the end product always a sorrow
of remorse or failure. I would give this anger
to Orion, whom I've only recently learned to identify,
forever on his back foot, his stories go
from bad to worse, and the benzene rises
like a prayer, arsenic on the breath
cold makes visible, that makes visible
the cold. A wider range of words exists
to describe effects of cold than heat.
Where somatosensory modalities are concerned
it's one of the more ambiguous precepts.
Being cold is not the same as feeling cold,
just as Seneca, who wrote on anger,
said it's different to know a thing
than to feel its truth. In the lab a single rat
restrained on a chill plate
will exhibit robust escape behaviour later
than will several others free
to shelter together in their enclosure
when temperature is slowly but drastically lowered —
I suppose with everything else going on
it can pretend it's not happening. Deception,
self-deception, advance by degrees,
my dead friend reminds me, and who hasn't

brought themselves to harm because
they thought they had to? The dead can be kinder
than the living, if you are not related to them.
The anger I would give Orion
is what has been given me, bitter shear
above the sea, empty pockets
planes fall through, and according to the Proverbs
to which I guiltily return,
sliding another out of its pack,
he who troubles his household with groundless anger
will inherit the chaos that some of us
truly seem to prefer. But Orion doesn't care
what anyone thinks and doesn't care
when this is weakness. Each day he pursues
what he considers his due
with a traitor's expectation of exacting fidelity,
no one more full of suspicion,
mistaking anger for courage, for reason,
and the same scorpion kills him.
One could try to filter anger
as a plant might, then through a coarsely woven
logic, then as would a machine
whose selling points are that it's cheap
and nearly silent, and still be
unequal to it, smoke rising
to Orion, and my friend, who was not immune
to anger, says I need to look past
the constellation, he can see farther than he ever has —
beyond the Horsehead Nebula, De Mairan's Nebula,
through hallways of the stellar nurseries,
beyond pattern (if it is pattern), and colour

(if it is colour), beyond narrative, he says, *Okay I'm being practical now, there is a clearing.*

MEADOWLARK

Prayer in the throat of a nonbeliever
offered up to the absent hereafter,
his two long notes and descending warble
put him at the centre of things.
A partial method, he knows, is no method;
and when you are too weak for beauty's
startlement, when you desire not silence
but the peace of vague and benign

neglect, at decibels audible over
the wind, radio, tires through gravel,
through the open driver's window
his song is like arrows of pure math
straight into whatever the heart is,
its still unbroken land, its native grasses.

STARCRAFT

The storm breaks down the day's last hour.
It slams through trees in the neighbour's garden
like air mechanically displaced
by compartments of another world sliding past
this one. Or another dimension. I like that better.
Still of this world, which includes both
what we know and can imagine. It would mean
you aren't gone, just out of frame, and might explain
this halfway sense of being neither here nor there:
where maybe, Dad, you and I, on the lake at dawn
when the fish jump, in the 14-foot aluminum Starcraft
and our contentment of few words, drift on water
calm and grey as a room risen into just before
it brightens, and I'm no longer frightened.

CANOPY

Anchored in shallow stony ditches
two cottonwoods built their circular staircases
80 feet high, around columns
of absolute nerve. In their shade
we'd make our fire to picnic
on the road allowance, which seems so strange
though at the time it was hardly a road
at all, no gas well trucks or corporate farms,
and it made us feel lucky and far away,
so few trees around, so little rain.
We learned the word 'canopy,' it was like
a miracle, owlets peering
through their nursery window to where we sat
on the graded dirt, and the smoke
from our hot dog fire rose straight up.
It was the same, Dad said,
when he was a child, owlets
in their canopy beds, time eddying
deep in the shelter of the cottonwoods
where demands of the yard and fields
couldn't enter, as though by a spell
we didn't cast but that welcomed us.
The heavy equipment passes
beneath them more often now,
edges of the widened road approach
yet they are there still, in excess

of their average lifespan
and function. In spring
they champagne the air with cotton.

NOTES

The title "That Which Was Learned in Youth Is Always Most Familiar" is adapted from Chapter 78 of the Icelandic saga of Grettir the Strong as it appears in the 1914 translation into English by G. H. Hight, accessed through the Icelandic Saga Database.

The italicized lines in "Red Spring" are from Virgil's *Eclogues* and *Georgics* in J. B. Greenough's translations.

"Caribou": Stillness in motion and motion in stillness are concepts articulated in Zen Buddhist philosophy through to quantum physics. "Out of weakness / are made strong" is from Hebrews 11: 33–34 (KJV).

In "Autumn Day," the italicized is from Stephen Mitchell's translation of Rainer Maria Rilke's "Herbstagg," or "Autumn Day," from *The Selected Poetry of Rainer Maria Rilke* (Vintage, 1989).

"On Faith": Peter Reveen was a hypnotist and illusionist who filled arenas across Canada in the late '70s and early '80s. Bret "The Hitman" Hart and Archie "The Stomper" Gouldie were stars of Stampede Wrestling, based in Calgary, Alberta.

"Las Cruces": Giovanni Maria de Agostini was born in Italy in 1801. A peripatetic solitary, he was arrested in Brazil for inspiring fanaticism, sent to an insane asylum in Mexico and then deported to Cuba. He lived above the Pecos Wilderness for three years in the 1860s and was murdered in 1869. A few members of the Sociedad del Ermitaño, or the Society of the Hermit, still exist.

"Dust" uses the story "Ole Lukøje" by Hans Christian Andersen, published in 1842, based on the European folklore of the Sandman. E. T. A. Hoffmann published a scarier version in 1816.

"Just Say the Word": On entering the palace of the Phaeacian king Alcinous, Odysseus marvels at the golden and silver dogs, immortal and un-aging, Hephaestus had fashioned to protect it *(Od. 7.91–94)*: Christopher A. Faraone writes that "the adjectives 'undying' and 'un-aging' refer not literally to biological life, but rather to the durability of the rust-proof metals from which they were fashioned, and that the dogs were alleged to be the work of Hephaestus solely on account of their excellent workmanship." ("Hephaestus the Magician and Near Eastern Parallels for Alcinous' Watchdogs." *Greek, Roman, and Byzantine Studies*. 28, no. 3 (2004): 257–80).

"Foxes": In 2020, Storm Dennis became one of the most intense extratropical cyclones ever recorded, exacerbating the extensive flooding and damage in England caused by Storm Ciara less than a week before.

"No One's Gonna Love You More than I Do" is a line from the song "No One's Gonna Love You" by Band of Horses, from 2007's *Cease to Begin*.

"The Mash": In the *Dictionary of Newfoundland English*, "The bogs (called locally 'mash') are simply peaty vegetation in various stages of decomposition — a typical muskeg."

The italicized final lines of "Mourning Doves" are from a traditional English folk song sung under the titles "Turtle Dove" and "Ten Thousand Miles," among others.

"The Grasslands": Grasslands National Park currently covers nearly 750 square kilometres in two blocks in southern Saskatchewan, bordering Montana. It is designated a Dark Sky Reserve by the Royal Astronomical Society of Canada.

"Smoke": 2023 was Canada's most destructive fire season on record, with 6.6 percent of the forested area in Alberta burned and 5 percent of the forest area in Canada.

Anne Dufourmantelle's books include *Défense du secret* (Manuels Payot, 2015), *Puissance de la douceur* (Payot, 2013), and *Eloge du Risque* (Payot, 2011).

"Prime Location" includes a line from "1948" by Denise Riley. The poem appears in *Lurex* (Picador, 2022).

"Orion": See *Anger, Mercy, Revenge* by Lucius Annaeus Seneca. Trans. Robert A. Kaster and Martha C. Nussbaum (University of Chicago Press, 2012). Also "The Molecular and Cellular Basis of Cold Sensation" by David D. McKemy in *ACS Chemical Neuroscience* 4, no. 2 (2013). According to Proverbs 11:29, "Whosoever troubles his own house will inherit the wind" (NKJV).

"Pines": Huddie William Ledbetter, songwriter and king of the 12-string guitar, was better known as Lead Belly.

ACKNOWLEDGEMENTS

Thank you to the editors of the following publications in which poems, in earlier versions, appeared: Academy of American Poets Poem-a-Day series, *Australian Book Review, BRAG, Free Bloody Birds, Harper's Magazine, Liberties, Literary Review of Canada, Poetry London, Sewanee Review, The Fiddlehead, The London Review of Books, The New York Review of Books, The Stinging Fly, The Telegraph* (UK), *The Times Literary Supplement,* and *The Walrus.*

Thank you Kevin Connolly, editor and friend, for knowing what really matters, and telling me. Thank you Colette Bryce, for your sensibility and discernment. Thank you Jonathan Galassi, for your invaluable support. My deep appreciation to everyone at House of Anansi Press, Picador, and Farrar, Straus and Giroux. And thanks to Peter Straus and RCW for taking me on.

"Red Spring," "The Grasslands," "Berkeley Hills, 2022," "The Barrens," and "Canopy" were commissioned for *Project Earth: Green Chapter,* a collaboration with Andrew Downing, Sarah Slean, and the Iris Trio: Christine Carter, Zoë Martin-Doike, and Anna Petrova. I'm honoured to be in your company. Christine, you are a perfect storm of talent, hard work, and generosity.

Thanks, too, to the patient and precise Nick Bonin.

Thank you to Mary Jo Salter, who selected "The Bluebird" for inclusion in *The Best American Poetry 2024.* And to Aislinn Hunter, who included "Flashlight" in *The Best Canadian Poetry 2025.*

Funding from the Canada Council for the Arts and Ontario Arts Council supported the completion of this book. A fellowship from the John Simon Guggenheim Memorial Foundation has allowed me to move on.

For ongoing camaraderie and support, thanks to my colleagues in the School of English at the University of St Andrews. Many of these poems were written during semesters at York University, University of California at Berkeley, Massey College at the University of Toronto, and Manchester Metropolitan University. Thanks especially to Robert Hass, Brenda Hillman, Smaro Kamboureli, Pasha Malla, Andrew McMillan, Michael Symmons Roberts, John Shoptaw, and Jean Sprackland. My gratitude also to Michael Hofmann, Ange Mlinko, Michael Ondaatje, and Srikanth Reddy.

For advice on the poems, warm company, and questionable jokes, thank you Lisa Brockwell, Niall Campbell, John Glenday, Lesley Harrison, Kathleen Jamie, and Don Paterson.

To my dear friends, who know who they are. It's been a long time now. I'm grateful for you every day.

The love, good sense, and stubborn humour of my family continues to be a blessing in the midst of our great loss.

This book is dedicated also to the memories of Stan Dragland, Steven Heighton, and John Burnside — writers and wanderers who, as Dad did, loved this world.